Volodymyr Zelenskyy

DEFENDER OF FREEDOM

L. D. Hicks

Post Hill Press
New York • Nashville
posthillpress.com

Published in the United States of America
1 2 3 4 5 6 7 8 9 10

*"Freedom is never more than
one generation away from extinction.
We didn't pass it to our children
in the bloodstream.
It must be fought for, protected,
and handed on for them to do the same."*

—RONALD REAGAN

In the early morning of February 24, 2022, an eerie silence hung over Kyiv, the capital city of Ukraine. Cloudy skies reflected the light from the city back down onto the buildings below. Security cameras among the skyscrapers and apartment buildings captured drivers on their way to work. Suddenly, air-raid sirens screamed a banshee wail that echoed through the streets. Thunderclaps and flashes of light in the distance were the first hints of the missile strikes and shelling launched by the Russian military. A full-scale invasion of Ukraine by Russia had begun.

Over 130,000 Russian tanks, troops, armored personnel carriers, anti-aircraft vehicles, missile launchers, and artillery rolled over the border. Missiles and rockets were launched at cities, military targets, and communication centers. Fighter jets launched missiles and dropped cluster bombs on cities and airports. Scores of civilians were killed and hundreds of apartments were destroyed, leaving thousands homeless. It was a full-scale assault by the Russian Federation—one of the world's superpowers—and it came across the border for one purpose only: to take away Ukrainians' freedom to decide what kind of country they wanted to live in.

Zelenskyy arrives in the Rivne region.

Within days—as the Russians attacked by land, sea, and air—women and children began a mass exodus from the major cities of Kyiv, Kherson, and Kharkiv, and hundreds of towns and villages. Cars and trucks clogged the highways in enormous traffic jams that stretched for miles. Train stations were packed with refugees as people tried to escape the war zones. Others were blocked from fleeing by constant warfare and shellfire, as Russia hit railway stations with cruise missiles. Like England during the Battle of Britain, citizens sheltered in metro stations and basements to hide from the explosions that were rocking their towns. Bodies littered the countryside, roads, and city blocks.

President Zelenskyy meets with servicemen of the State Border Guard Service.

But something else was happening. All across the country, the citizens who had stayed behind were stirring. Relief agencies began gathering clothing, food, and medicine to rush to areas affected by the fighting. The Ukrainian army and air forces rushed to meet their Russian counterparts where they could. Entire Russian tank columns were destroyed by shoulder-fired missiles and whatever fighter jets Ukraine could send up into the skies.

Resistance stiffened and became fierce. Videos of Ukrainian citizens standing in front of tanks populated the internet. Local breweries stopped brewing beer and began brewing Molotov cocktails.

Massive blood drives were organized and—like something out of a black and white newsreel after Pearl Harbor—thousands of men and women flocked to recruiting stations to join the Ukrainian military. The government made it legal for any civilian to use a weapon to defend their country, and school teachers, bankers, and farmers took up arms.

Women's groups tore apart old clothing and began weaving camouflage netting to hide Ukrainian combat units, mobile hospitals, and other military assets. Girls with purple nail polish learned to strip and clean assault rifles, and were trained in first aid and urban combat. Other volunteers made sandbags and "hedgehogs" of steel girders and railroad ties to block Russian tanks from advancing.

Zelenskyy visits with frontline military positions in the Dotesk region.

> ### "When you attack us, you will see our faces. Not our backs, but our faces."[*]
>
> —VOLODYMYR ZELENSKYY

* Volodymyr Zelenskyy, "Full transcript of Zelenskyy's emotional appeal to Russians," NBC News, February 24, 2022. www.nbcnews.com/news/world/full-transcript-zelenskyys-emotional-appeal-russians-rcna17485.

President Zelenskyy visits soldiers in the Kharkiv region.

Elderly women stood in the streets berating Russian soldiers: *"Go home!"* and *"Your mothers would be ashamed of you!"* Citizens blocked the streets with their bodies, preventing resupply convoys from getting to their destinations. A man was run over by a tank as he tried to block it from moving up a street.

Where did this fighting spirit come from? How did this patriotic desire for freedom become focused and begin to flourish? Why did citizens fight back as well as cower in the debris of their homes? What gave Ukrainians the inspiration to stand up and fight the invader against overwhelming odds?

Left, below & opposite: *President Zelenskyy surveys war destruction in the Kharkiv region.*

President Zelenskyy surveys war damage in the Kyiv region.

President Zelenskyy addresses the media in the Kyiv region.

President Zelenskyy shares a solemn moment with servicemen in the Zaporizhzhia region near Donbas.

Volodymyr Zelenskyy was born to Jewish parents on January 25, 1978, in the industrial city of Kryvyy Rih, Ukraine—known for iron and uranium mining, and steel and drill manufacturing—in what was then the Union of Soviet Socialist Republics (U.S.S.R.). Soon after his birth, his family moved to Mongolia, where his father, Oleksandr, worked as a computer science and cybernetics professor and his mother, Rymma, as an engineer. After four years, Zelenskyy and his mother returned to Kryvyy Rih, where she retired from engineering due to health problems caused by the harsh climate of Mongolia. His father remained in Mongolia, working as a Soviet specialist helping to build a mining and processing plant.[1]

---

1 Gordon Exclusive, interview with Vladimir Zelenskyy, "If I am Elected president, they will first pour mud on me, then respect me, and then cry when I leave." M.gordonua.com.

Like many Ukrainians, Zelenskyy grew up speaking Russian, with Ukrainian his second language. At school, he studied law with the goal of becoming a diplomat. He won a competition after scoring well on an academic English fluency test and received a grant to go to school in Israel, but his father would not let him leave the country. Zelenskyy ended up at the Kryvyy Rih Institute of Economics, and received a degree in law in 2000.

However, Zelenskyy was more attracted to show business than the law. Before graduating high school, he began to participate in an organization that would eventually lead him to the presidency of Ukraine and the center of a global firestorm—his local KVN comedy competition team.

President Zelenskyy and the Prime Minister of the United Kingdom meeting in Kyiv.

President Zelenskyy meets with the Presidents of France and Romania, the Chancellor of Germany, and the Prime Minister of Italy.

KVN is a Ukrainian acronym for *Klub vesyólykh i nakhódchivykh,*[2] a title that translates into English as "the Club of the Funny and Inventive People." A game show created for Soviet TV in 1961,[3] it is a combination of—in American terms—*Politically Incorrect, Saturday Night Live, Second City,* and *Whose Line Is It Anyway?,* with a dash of *American Idol.* Teams of mostly university students are pitted against each other in a battle of wits, combining singing and dancing, satire, and intellectual improvisation, and scored with a complicated system by celebrity judges.

2 Michael Ray, "Volodymyr Zelenskyy," *Encyclopedia Britannica,* May 4, 2022. www.britannica.com/biography/Volodymyr-Zelensky.

3 Vadim Goloperov, "KVN and Odessa: Between Humor and Politics," *Odessa Review,* April 1, 2016. odessareview.com/kvn-odessa-humor-politics/

The KVN teams were originally only inside the Soviet Union, until the whole competition was shut down in 1972 by Soviet censors who found the political humor offensive. However, KVN was brought back in 1986, and now teams from all over Europe, Israel, and even the United States compete for the championship. As with *American Idol* or *Saturday Night Live*, KVN players can become celebrities, movie stars, and—in Zelenskyy's case—President of Ukraine.

Zelenskyy was recognized as a rising star and was asked to join the United Ukrainian team soon after joining his regional league at the tender age of seventeen, which won the competition in 1997.

Originally a dancer, Zelenskyy soon began to get acting roles. As his star rose, he founded his own team: the Kvartal 95, named after "the 95th Quarter," the neighborhood in central Kryvyy Rih where he grew up. He was their creative heart as well as their captain,

writing most of their skits. Kvartal 95 toured frequently, and produced programs on the national Ukrainian television network 1+1.[4]

The future president was also the voice of Paddington Bear in the Ukrainian versions of *Paddington* and *Paddington 2*. The final broadcast of *Dancing with the Stars*—in which Zelenskyy won, voted the fan favorite by viewers—had better ratings than the inaugural New Year's address of the new president of Ukraine.[5]

By then, Volodymyr Zelenskyy was the hottest performer in the country's entertainment industry, starring in movies as well as TV programs, commercials, and theater. The foundation of his humor was wicked satire in the mode of Benny Hill, poking fun at

President Zelenskyy meets with the Prime Ministers of Albania, Montenegro, and North Macedonia.

4   Nita A. Ocbe, "Zelenskyy Vladimir: Project Manager 'Kvartal-95,'" October 28, 2011. web.archive.org/web/20190102050545/ file.liga.net/persons/vladimir-zelenskii.

5   Michael Ray, "Volodymyr Zelenskyy," *Encyclopedia Britannica*, May 4, 2022. www.britannica.com/biography/Volodymyr-Zelensky.

President Zelenskyy meets with the President of the European Commission in Kyiv.

Ukrainian and Russian politicians and the rampant corruption of the oligarchs. The humor rang true with millions of Ukrainians, who appreciated the courage it takes to buck the system in Eastern Europe where Vladimir Putin, dictator of the local superpower, enforces his will on the region by targeted assassinations.[6]

Zelenskyy entered politics via a television show he created, *Servant of the People,* a satire of Ukrainian politics similar to American comedies like *Dave, Veep,* and *The West Wing.* He played a

high school history teacher who becomes the president of Ukraine after his students put his rant against political corruption on YouTube. It ran for four seasons, becoming the most popular show in Ukraine (and is now carried by Netflix around the world). In *Servant of the People,* the unlikely new president has to navigate the comedic world of bloated luxury bought and paid for by oligarchic corruption. Exasperated by the status quo, he elevates his close friends to be his advisors and cabinet members, who also navigate their new world in a comedic excess of epic proportions.

6 "List of Soviet and Russian assassinations," Wikipedia. en.wikipedia.org/wiki/List_of_Soviet_and_Russian_assassinations.

May 22, 2022

22 травня 2022 року

President Zelenskyy meets the President of the Republic of Poland in Kyiv.

The show's anti-corruption message resonated with the Ukrainian people, and Zelenskyy's production company registered *Servant of the People* as a political party. Meanwhile, the economy was in and the approval rating of the latest billionaire president was sinking. Zelenskyy threw his hat into the electoral ring, and—as with all of his successful endeavors—emerged as the front runner in the presidential race.[7]

On April 21, 2019, Volodymyr Zelenskyy was elected president of Ukraine with 73 percent of the vote. As life imitated the art of his television show, the political amateur with reformist ideals was sworn in on May 19, 2019, and was immediately thrust into a world where government decisions were not satirical comedy, but affected the lives of millions. Zelenskyy's ideals and character would be put to the test. Ukraine would be pressured by the imperialist designs of the Russian Federation. The European Union and the United States would

---

7   Michael Ray, "Volodymyr Zelenskyy," *Encyclopedia Britannica*, March 25, 2022. www.britannica.com/biography/VolodyrZelenskyy.

demand corruption reform. Zelenskyy's own people would demand that he live up to his campaign promises. When Russia launched its invasion of Ukraine in 2022, the comedian-turned-president would be forged by the fires of war into a defender of freedom.

Ukraine is the second largest country in Europe, after Russia. It is bordered by Poland, Slovakia, and Hungary to the west; Belarus to the north; Romania, Moldova, and the Black Sea to the south; and Russia to the east. As the crossroad between East and West, Ukraine has been fought over and dominated by imperialist powers for six hundred years, ruled at different times by Poland, the Ottoman Empire, and Tsarist Russia.

In the 20th century, the Soviet Union absorbed Ukraine, and in 1932 proceeded to destroy its rebellious population by confiscating crops and killing cattle, deliberately causing a famine that starved millions of people. During World War II, the Nazis

President Zelenskyy meets the Prime Minister of Portugal.

Zelenskyy meets with the Chairpersons of both Houses of the Irish Parliament.

massacred thousands more on their way to the Soviet Union, including most of Volodymyr Zelenskyy's Jewish family, who were killed when the Nazis burned their village. His grandfather and all of his brothers had joined the Soviet Red Army, but only his grandfather survived the war.

Ukraine only became a fully independent nation after the collapse of the Soviet Union. In 1991, the legislature of the Ukrainian Soviet Socialist Republic claimed independence, renamed itself Ukraine, and a few months later a national referendum overwhelmingly approved the decision. However, Ukraine had hurdles to overcome once it became an independent nation: nuclear disarmament, control of the Crimea and the Black Sea ports, and relations with the primarily ethnic Russian population of several territories on the Russian border.

Ambassadors of foreign countries to Ukraine present credentials to President Zelenskyy.

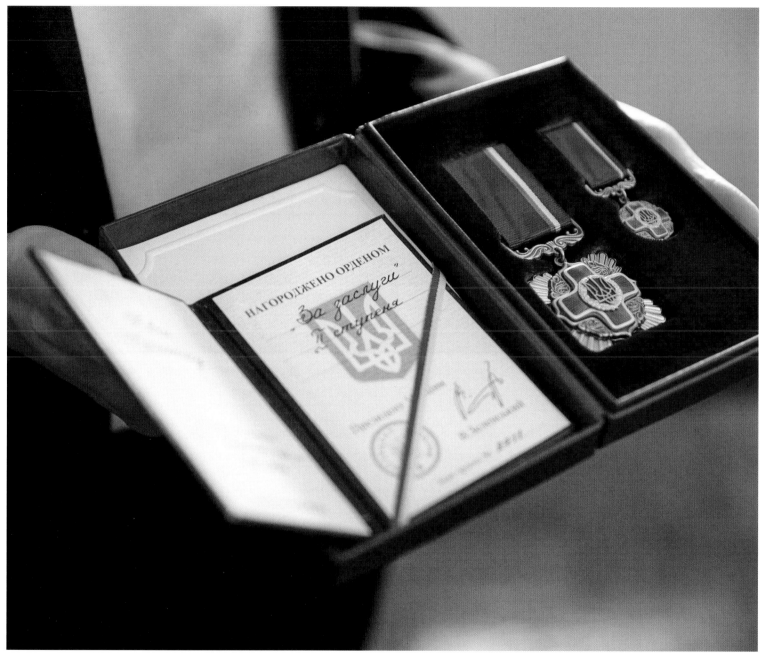

The credentials presented to President Zelenskyy.

Ukraine set up its own military, claimed the Crimea, and established territorial control over the disputed border areas. Its citizens looked to Western Europe and the United States as role models of freedom and democracy, and the government founded a pro-Western—rather than pro-Russian—diplomatic service. Ukraine began to express a desire to join the European Union.

After independence, Ukraine found itself the third largest nuclear power in the world. The population had mixed feelings about nuclear energy after the horrifying nuclear plant meltdown at Chernobyl in April of 1986. The government did not want the cost of maintaining the weapons, nor the political pressure from the international community, which ordered the country to dismantle those weapons and ship them to Russia.

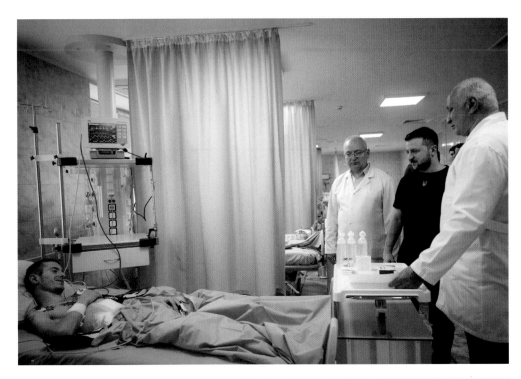

Zelenskyy visits the Shalimov National Institute of Surgery and Transplantology.

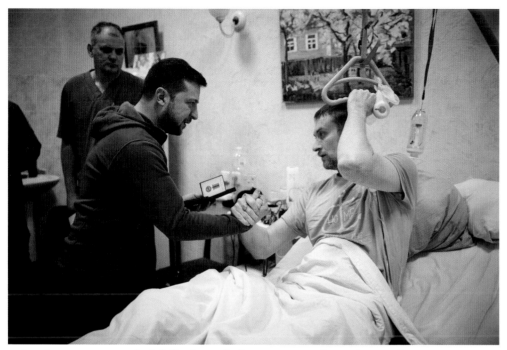

Zelenskyy visits wounded defenders of Ukraine at a military hospital.

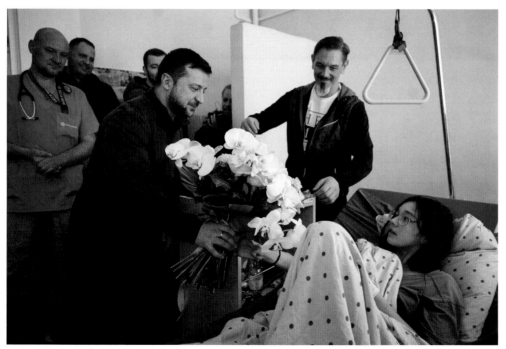

President Zelenskyy visits residents of Kyiv, wounded by enemy shelling.

However, Russia began claiming the disputed areas with Russian ethnic populations. In Putin's view, Ukraine was still an integral part of Russia, and any assertion of independence must be due to foreign influence rather than the desire of the Ukrainian people. After World War II, the Soviet Union had not freed the countries it had liberated from Nazi Germany, but had lowered the Iron Curtain, turning former nations and ethnic communities into vassal states. Putin, as a former KGB agent, wanted to reclaim as much of the former Soviet empire as he could.

The Ukrainian government began to have second thoughts about shipping the warheads back to what it was beginning to consider a hostile neighbor. They halted the arms shipments to demand guarantees for security and financial compensation for the cost of disarmament.[8]

8   Ivan Alekseyevich Yerofeyev, "Ukraine," *Encyclopedia Britannica*, March 2, 2022. www.britannica.com/place/Ukraine.

President Zelenskyy participates in an event commemorating the 36th anniversary of the Chornobyl tragedy.

Suddenly, and for the first time, Ukraine found itself squeezed between the hostility of Russia and the demands of the West. Ukraine was branded a rogue nation by the United States, bringing intense diplomatic pressure to bear on the new nation. However, the United States acceded to Ukrainian demands for guarantees and brokered "security assurances" in which Russia guaranteed the sovereignty of Ukraine, promising to "refrain from the threat or use of force against the territorial integrity or political independence of Ukraine."[9] Ukraine then completed the transfer of its nuclear weapons to Russia.

Over the next decade, Ukraine grew as a nation, its people battling corruption, a weak economy, and the hostility of Russia. Disputed elections between pro-Russian and pro-Western candidates

9 Editorial Board, "How Ukraine Was Betrayed in Budapest," *Wall Street Journal*, February 23, 2022. www.wsj.com/articles/how-ukraine-was-betrayed-in-budapest-russia-vladimir-putin-us-uk-volodymyr-zelensky-nuclear-weapons-11645657263.

President Zelenskyy participates in events on the Journalist's Day.

for prime minister triggered protests and riots, in what was called the Orange Revolution. For several years, hundreds were killed in the street fighting, as rival factions battled over whether Ukraine should strengthen ties with the West or with Russia. Prime ministers came and went, and the relationship with the West grew stronger, much to the consternation of Vladimir Putin.[10]

In 2014, after savagely invading several other former vassal states of the Soviet Union, Putin turned his attention to reclaiming a Ukraine weakened by internal conflict and separatist efforts on the Russian border. Echoing Adolf Hitler's takeover of the Sudetenland, Putin first invaded the Crimea—blatantly violating Russia's previous agreements to respect Ukraine's sovereignty—on the pretext that its mostly Russian populace needed protection from Ukrainian oppression.

---

10   "Ukraine crisis: Timeline," BBC, November 13, 2014. www.bbc.com/news/world-middle-east-26248275.

Zelenskyy on a working visit to the Mykolaiv and Odesa regions.

Then Russia armed separatists in the Donbas state on the Russian border, who took over local government offices and military bases, but denied its own involvement in what it called an internal Ukrainian matter. Ukraine fought back and looked to the West for aid, and damaging economic sanctions were imposed on Russia, but to no avail. Further turmoil ensued as the people of this beleaguered nation continued to look for a leader who would sponsor reforms instead of participating in political corruption. Sensing weakness, Russia pressed harder, sending more weapons and troops into the disputed areas. These were the dilemmas Volodymyr Zelenskyy was elected to solve.

President Zelenskyy greets the Prime Minister of Luxembourg in Kyiv.

President Zelenskyy presents awards to servicemen who have conferred the title of Hero of Ukraine.

During World War II, Franklin D. Roosevelt broadcast "fireside chats" over the radio to keep his fellow Americans informed about the course of the war. Winston Churchill made radio addresses to inspire his people, who were being bombed every day by the Nazis. Volodymyr Zelenskyy's tool is the smartphone, which enables him to speak directly to Ukrainians—and the rest of the world—through social media networks. Having run an unorthodox presidential campaign by avoiding mainstream journalists, candidate debates, and campaign rallies in favor of YouTube videos and Kvartal 95 comedy routines, he was already used to seeing the public as his audience and communicating directly with them.[11] He is the first war time national leader in the age of social media.

When Russian propaganda units tried to spread rumors that Zelenskyy had fled the country or was in hiding, he posted a video of himself standing in the middle of Kyiv. Surrounded by advisors, he said, "I am here. We are not putting down arms. We will be defending our country, because our weapon is truth. And our truth is that this is our land, our country, our children, and we will defend all this. That is it, that's all I wanted to tell you. Glory to Ukraine!" After this rousing speech, "I am here!" and "Glory to Ukraine!" became the battle cries of the beleaguered nation.

Earlier that day, with the Russian army advancing toward the capital, the United States had offered President Zelenskyy assistance to evacuate himself and his family, to avoid them being captured or killed by Russian military forces. Zelenskyy's reply went viral all over the world: "The fight is here—I need ammunition, not a ride!"

11 Adrian Karatnycky, "The World Just Witnessed the First Entirely Virtual Presidential Campaign," Politico, April 24, 2019. web.archive.org/web/20190425131841. www.politico.com/magazine/story/2019/04/24/ukraine-president-virtual-campaign-226711.

Zelenskyy meets with AFU servicemen who were awarded the title Hero of Ukraine.

Later that evening, in a bunker, the president gave a speech to the nation and the world. Standing behind the podium in an olive drab t-shirt, with fierce determination in his eyes, Zelenskyy called for the world to aid Ukraine in its moment of crisis. He said that he had tried to call Vladimir Putin and had received silence in reply. Now, Zelenskyy spoke directly to the Russian people:

> *"We know for sure that we don't need the war. Not a Cold War, not a hot war. Not a hybrid one. But if we'll be attacked by the enemy troops, if they try to take our country away from us, our freedom, our lives, the lives of our children, we will defend ourselves. Not attack, but defend ourselves. And when you will be attacking us, you will see our faces, not our backs, but our faces."*[12]

The defender of freedom had taken a stand and set an example for the people of Ukraine. The target was on all of their backs. If they would stay and fight, so would he. "I am not afraid of anyone," he said. "For as long as it takes to win this war, I'm staying in Kyiv."

His personal bravery established, Zelenskyy roamed the city in a khaki t-shirt and occasionally body armor with a helmet, talking to the soldiers on the front lines as the Russian forces advanced toward the capital, visiting both wounded soldiers and citizens in the hospitals, and giving out medals.

---

12 Volodymyr Zelenskyy, "Full transcript of Zelenskyy's emotional appeal to Russians," NBC News, February 24, 2022. www.nbcnews.com/news/world/full-transcript-zelenskyys-emotional-appeal-russians-rcna17485.

Zelenskyy distributes state awards to servicemen of the Armed Forces of Ukraine and the families of fallen defenders.

He exhorted his countrymen:

"What can Ukrainians do? Help the national defense. Join the ranks of the Armed Forces of Ukraine and the territorial defense units. Any citizen with combat experience will now be useful. It is up to you and all of us whether the enemy will be able to advance further into the territory of our independent state."[13]

He was in constant contact with his advisors, the troops—who were hunkered down in their besieged bunkers begging for more weapons[14]—and with his wife and children, who had been evacuated after the war began. Dark circles blossomed under his eyes. His bodyguards were terrified that a Russian sniper would shoot him; it was rumored that Russian special forces squadrons and sabotage units were being parachuted into the capital just to assassinate him and capture or kill his wife and children. "The enemy has marked me as target number one, my family number two," he said. "They want to destroy Ukraine politically by destroying the head of state." He told European leaders in a video call, "This may be the last time you see me alive."

Russian missile strikes continued to devastate civilian infrastructure—housing, schools, hospitals, and playgrounds. The cityscapes of Ukraine looked like war-torn cities from World War II photographs, but in high-definition color: apartment blocks burnt black and crumbling, smoke rising, curtains and shutters hanging down from blasted window

---

13 "Ukraine's President: We Are 'Handing Out Weapons' to 'Everyone Who Wants' to Defend Ukraine," CNS News, February 24, 2022. cnsnews.com/blog/cnsnewscom-staff-writer/ukraines-president-we-are-handing-out-weapons-everyone-who-wants.

14 Simon Shuster, "Inside Zelensky's World," *Time Magazine*, April 28, 2022. time.com/6171277/volodymyr-Zelenskyy-interview-ukraine-war/.

President Volodymyr Zelenskyy meets President of the European Council Charles Michel in Kyiv.

sills, crumpled radio towers lying on the ground, streets strewn with bricks and exploded vehicles. Blackouts were imposed on all cities (that is, when the electricity worked, since utilities were one of Russia's primary targets) in order to be invisible to Russian missiles.

The Russian strategy became obvious. The Ukrainian army was putting up too strong a defense, so Russia would pursue a scorched earth policy, destroying homes and killing civilians instead. If the army would not surrender, perhaps the people of Ukraine would. If the infrastructure of the country was destroyed, a devastated Ukraine would pose no threat to Vladimir Putin, even if Russia was eventually forced to leave. Despite this, the resolve of Zelenskyy and his fellow countrymen only grew fiercer as they became more determined to drive the Russians out.

Over the years, the European Union and the United States had been supplying arms and supplies in piecemeal fashion, concerned about how Putin would respond along with the worldwide consequences of supporting Ukraine. For example, the Russian Federation not only retains thousands of nuclear weapons, but supplies a huge amount of oil and natural gas to much of the European Union, and grain to the rest of the world. As the Russian military began massing on the borders of Zelenskyy's beleaguered country, more aid was delivered but—despite the United States delivering constant intelligence updates to Ukraine of imminent invasion—there was still no sense of urgency. This was about to change.

Zelenskyy began to rally the West in the same way as he had inspired his own countrymen, with his iron determination and actor's communication

President Zelenskyy participates in celebrations on the 30th anniversary of the Department of State Protection.

skills. He addressed ten European parliaments in two weeks, each time receiving a standing ovation. Appearing by video before an emergency meeting of European leaders, he gave an impassioned plea for help, which moved his translator to tears, and convinced Germany, Hungary, and Italy to impose tougher economic sanctions on the Russian Federation.

He was direct and to the point with Western leaders, eschewing diplomatic phrases but crafting each speech to play on the emotions of the audience. To the United Kingdom, he referenced Shakespeare and the Battle of Britain, when the Nazis were bombing England daily. He paraphrased one of Winston Churchill's greatest speeches,

inserting Ukrainian geography: "We shall fight in the woods, in the fields, on the beaches, in the cities, and villages, in the streets, we shall fight in the hills."[15]

Addressing the United States, he referenced the Japanese sneak attack on Pearl Harbor and Martin Luther King Jr.'s "I Have a Dream" speech, saying his dream was for America to protect the sky. He showed videos of the dead and wounded from Russian missile strikes, told the politicians that Ukrainians were experiencing September 11th every day, and then asked for a no-fly zone, fighter jets, and air defense systems…

15   Paul Adams, "'Shame on You': How President Zelensky Uses Speeches to Get What He Needs," March 24, 2022, BBC News. www.bbc.com/news/world-europe-60855280.

President Zelenskyy meets with the President of the Republic of Azerbaijan.

"Today, the Ukrainian people are not only defending Ukraine. We are fighting for the values of Europe and the world, sacrificing our lives in the name of the future. That's why today the American people are helping not just Ukraine, but Europe and the world to keep the planet alive. To keep justice in history. Now I'm almost forty-five years old. Today, my age stopped. When the hearts of more than one hundred children stopped beating. I see no sense in life if it cannot stop the deaths. And this is my main issue as the leader of my people. Brave Ukrainians. And as the leader of my nation, I am addressing President Biden. You are the leader of your great nation. I wish you to be the leader of the world. Being the leader of the world means to be the leader of peace. Thank you."[16]

He warned of a new Iron Curtain descending over Eastern Europe, reminding the United States that during the Cold War it had fought two wars in Asia based on the Domino Theory:[17] after one country fell to communism, then the one on its border, and then the next, would fall like dominos. If Ukraine fell, who would be next? Poland? Germany? France? Hungary? Would Europe and the world allow Ukraine to become the first domino to fall in Europe?

---

16 Volodymyr Zelenskyy, "Transcript of Volodymyr Zelenskyy's speech to the US Congress," March 16, 2022. www.msn.com/en-us/news/world/transcript-of-volodymyr-zelenskyys-speech-to-the-us-congress/ar-AAV8IYs.

17 "Domino Theory," *Encyclopedia Britannica*, www.britannica.com/topic/domino-theory.

Defender of Freedom | 33

Zelenskyy awards KORD fighters who maintain law and order during the Russian invasion.

For years, the West had been calling on Russia and its former republics to become democratic, to embrace freedom as a way of life for their citizens. Well, Ukraine had now thrown out the corrupt presidents and oligarchs that had been ruining the country for almost thirty years, and its citizens were doing their best to make their country a better place to live. For their troubles, they were being killed and their country destroyed. What was the West going to do about it?

Zelenskyy and his media advisors—masters of memes, tweets, and TikToks—were able to get his message out all over the world, garnering massive support from civilians in countries as far away as Japan and Israel. A week after the invasion, he broadcast a message of solidarity to the people of Europe on Zoom, on video screens set up in their town squares:

> *"Don't turn a blind eye on this. Come out and support Ukraine as much as you can. If we fall you fall. And if we win, and I'm sure we'll win, this will be the victory of our freedom, this will be the victory of light over darkness, of freedom over slavery. And if we win we will become as blossoming as Europe. And Europe will be flourishing more than ever. All of you are Ukrainians today, thank you for this."*[18]

18 Dennis Wagner, "Volodymyr Zelenskyy delivers rousing speech," *Times of News*, March 5, 2022. usa.timesofnews.com/city/hawaii/volodymyr-zelenskyy-delivers-rousing-speech-former-vp-mike-pence-warns-gop-live-updates.html.

President Zelenskyy attends ceremony honoring the memory of the Heroes of Kruty.

Western governments began sending more food, medicine, clothing, and arms in massive quantities: ammunition, shoulder-fired rockets, surface-to-air missile systems, drones, anti-tank weapons, and communication equipment. Food and blood drives sprang up across Poland and Germany.

So many foreign citizens flocked to Ukraine to join the fight that some had to be turned away, because there were not yet enough weapons for them. The European Union gave refugees legal status. (Poland, perhaps remembering its own misery under the Soviet boot, has been especially generous to displaced Ukrainians.)

The United States had initially settled on escalating sanctions based on Russia's behavior, but quickly changed its tune as Ukraine's stubborn military began to push back Russian tank columns.

Russian assets were frozen, trade shut down, restrictions on Russian banks and oil and gas imports were established and enforced, and billions of dollars were allocated for aid and arms.

As this book goes to press in mid-2022, the war continues. Worries grow over widening conflict and the possibility of a nuclear exchange; territory is taken and retaken by each combatant. Peace talks have been suggested but not achieved; war crimes by both combatants are alleged and documented. Sanctions have escalated, decades-old alliances and neutralities are shifting, and grain and oil exports from both combatants have been blocked, causing fears of famine and freezing. Hundreds of thousands have escaped the war zones through humanitarian corridors, although some convoys have been blocked. Over five million people have been displaced inside Ukraine's

Zelenskyy visits the Kharkiv and Dontsk regions.

borders, and more than two million people—mostly women, children, and elderly—have actually left the country. Europe has not seen such a disaster since World War II.

In spite of all this, Ukrainian morale is still high and determination still intense. Volodymyr Zelenskyy and Ukraine are now the tip of the spear for the defense of freedom in the world. Massive protests have broken out in Russia against the war.[19] Although Putin has continued the Soviet practice of secret police arresting protestors and opposition leaders,[20] Zelenskyy has inspired Russians as well as his own people to demand freedom. For years,

China has wanted to absorb Taiwan the same way Putin covets Ukraine. Seeing the firestorm of international outrage caused by the invasion of Ukraine—and how sanctions and trade regulations have damaged the Russian Federation—China may be having second thoughts.

Meanwhile, in the West, citizens who had become complacent about their borders and defense capabilities—taking for granted the lives their forefathers gave to fight and die for freedom—may be waking up.

Volodymyr Zelenskyy and Ukraine are reminding us that freedom should never be taken for granted and that defending it comes with a cost.

Glory to Ukraine! I am here!

19 Chris Pleasance, "Thousands chant 'f*** the war' at a concert in St Petersburg as Putin faces backlash over Ukrainian invasion," *Daily Mail*, May 23, 2022. www.dailymail.co.uk/news/article-10844695/Ukraine-Thousands-chant-f-war-concert-Russia.html.

20 Sarah Rainsford, "Ukraine war: The defiant Russians speaking out about the war," BBC, May 23, 2022. www.bbc.com/news/world-europe-61542365.

President Zelenskyy visits a food bank in Bucha, outside of Kyiv.

"We shall fight in the woods, in the fields, on the beaches, in the cities, and villages, in the streets, we shall fight in the hills."

—VOLODYMYR ZELENSKYY

President Zelenskyy praises servicemen that serve close to the front line in the Donetsk region.

Zelenskyy meets with servicemen of the State Service of Special Communication and Information Protection of Ukraine.

Zelenskyy meets with the President of the European Commission and the High Representative of the EU for Foreign Affairs and Security Policy.

Zelenskyy meets with a delegation of the U.S. Senate.

> *"The president can't change the country on his own. But what can he do? He can give an example."*
>
> —VOLODYMYR ZELENSKYY

President Zelenskyy meets the Speaker of the U.S. House of Representatives.

Zelenskyy meets with the President of Lithuania and the President of Poland.

Zelenskyy meets with the President of European Parliament.

Zelenskyy meets with Head of the Delegation of the European Union to Ukraine Matti Maasikas.

Zelenskyy meets with the Foreign Ministers of Germany and the Netherlands.

> *"I do not try to play a role. I feel good being myself and saying what I think."*

—VOLODYMYR ZELENSKYY

President Zelenskyy participates in the solemn raising of the State Flag on the Day of Unity.

President Zelenskyy meets with the UN Secretary-General.

President Zelenskyy meets with the U.S. Secretary of Defense and Secretary of State.

President Zelenskyy and the First Lady participate in the ceremony of sending off the national team of Ukraine to the XVI Summer Paralympic Games.

"*I would never want Ukraine
to be a piece on the map,
on the chessboard of big global players,
so that someone could toss us around,
use us as cover,
as part of some bargain.*"

—VOLODYMYR ZELENSKYY

President Zelenskyy meets the Prime Minister of Croatia.

President Zelenskyy meets the Prime Minister of Romania in Kyiv.

President Zelenskyy meets with the Prime Minister of Bulgaria.

President Zelenskyy and the First Lady celebrate the Day of the Diplomatic Service of Ukraine.

> # "There is nothing impossible to him who will try."
>
> —ALEXANDER THE GREAT

President Zelenskyy participates in the third Diia Summit.

President Zelenskyy meets with the winners of the all-Ukrainian competition Ukraine NOW.

President Zelenskyy meets the Prime Ministers of Spain and Denmark.

Zelenskyy meets with foreign journalists.

Zelenskyy at a press conference with representatives of foreign media.

President Zelenskyy addresses foreign journalists.

President Zelenskyy meets with the U.S. Secretary of State.

President Zelenskyy meets with the President of the Slovak Republic in Kyiv.

President Zelenskyy at the presentation of state awards to servicemen and families of fallen Heroes of Ukraine.

President Zelenskyy meets with the Prime Ministers of Albania and Montenegro.

"If there is no Ukrainian strong army,
there will be no Ukraine, and that will be the case
when everyone will understand…
it's not the war in Ukraine, it's the war in Europe.
We are defending our country, our land.
We are not attacking anyone,
because that is immoral."

—VOLODYMYR ZELENSKYY

President Zelenskyy arrives by helicopter to the Mykolaiv and Odesa regions.

Zelenskyy participates in events on the Day of Foreign Intelligence of Ukraine.

Zelenskyy meets with the President of France.

Zelenskyy meets the Minister of Foreign Affairs of Denmark.

Zelenskyy meets with the Prime Minister of the Netherlands.

President Zelenskyy meets with the President of the Republic of Turkey.

Zelenskyy monitors the launch of a Ukrainian satellite into orbit.

Zelenskyy meets the Federal Chancellor of Austria.

Right & below:
Zelenskyy participates in the events on the occasion of the Day of Liberation of Kyiv from Nazi Invaders.

Zelenskyy meets with EBA members.

Zelenskyy visits the Kharkiv region.

Zelenskyy meets with representatives of the All-Ukrainian Council of Churches.

Zelenskyy speaking at an event for international and Ukrainian media.

Zelenskyy attends the meeting of the Congress of Local and Regional Authorities.

President Zelenskyy meets with cadets and lyceum students of military educational institutions in Ukraine.

Zelenskyy participates in the events of International Volunteer Day.

Zelenskyy awards NGU servicemen on the Day of the National Guard of Ukraine.

Zelenskyy meets with representatives of Apple Inc.

Zelenskyy presents the Golden Star Order to the families of fallen servicemen.

President Zelenskyy at the opening of the Ukrainian-Polish intergovernmental consultations.

President Zelenskyy with the Prime Minister of Canada.

President Zelenskyy visits the Okhmatdyt Children's Hospital.

Zelenskyy visits the Central for Pediatric Cardiology and Cardiac Surgery in Kyiv.

Zelenskyy participates in the 58th Munich Security Conference in Germany.

President Zelenskyy and the First Lady honor the memory of the Holodomor victims.

Left & opposite: *President Zelenskyy and the First Lady attend the opening of the New Year's town.*

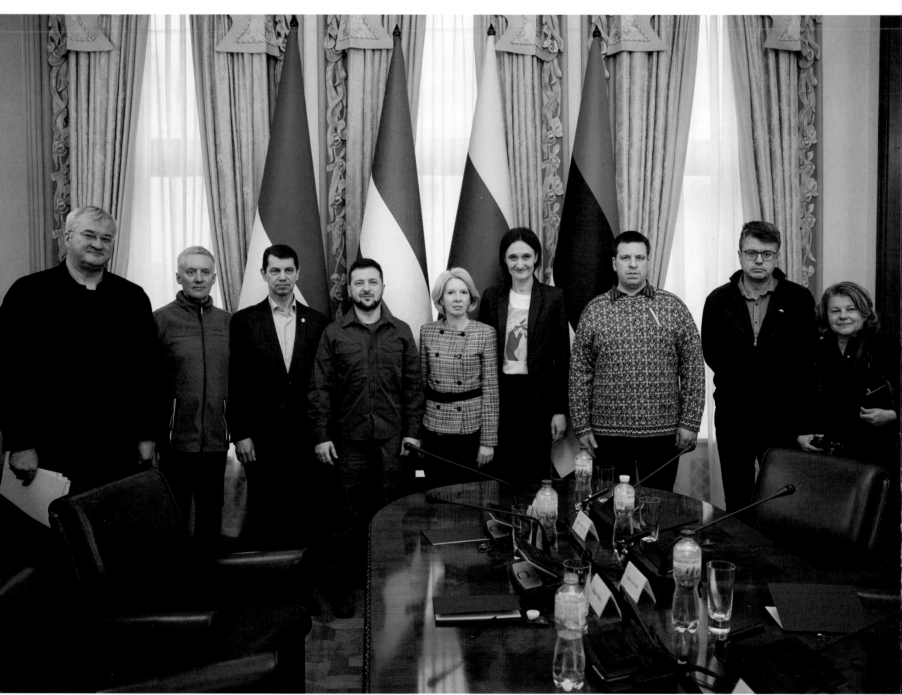

Zelenskyy meets with Speakers of the Parliaments of Lithuania, Latvia, and Estonia.